Morris Magpie

Favourite verse by
LYDIA PENDER

Morning Magpie

Illustrated by Noela Young

ANGUS
& ROBERTSON
PUBLISHERS

*Many of the poems in this
collection were originally
published in* Marbles in My
Pocket *(1957)*, Brown Paper
Leaves *(1971) and* The School
Magazine.

*Publication assisted by the
Literature Board of the Australia Council,
the Federal Government's arts funding
and advisory body.*

ANGUS & ROBERTSON PUBLISHERS

*Unit 4, Eden Park, 31 Waterloo Road,
North Ryde, NSW, Australia 2113, and
16 Golden Square, London W1R 4BN,
United Kingdom*

*First published in Australia
by Angus & Robertson Publishers in 1984
First published in the United Kingdom
by Angus & Robertson (UK) in 1984
This Bluegum paperback edition 1987*

*National Library of Australia
Cataloguing-in-publication data.*

*Pender, Lydia, 1907-
   Morning magpie.*

   ISBN 0 207 15572 0 (pbk.).

   *1. Children's poetry, Australian. I. Young, Noela, II.
   Title. (Series: Bluegum).*

A821'.3

*Typeset in 12pt Goudy Old Style Roman
Printed in Australia*

CONTENTS

From *Brown Paper Leaves*

More Recent Verse

To Nuri Mass
*in affectionate acknowledgement
of a continuing debt*

FOREWORD

It all began because Alison had tonsillitis. Alison is my younger daughter — the third child in a family of four. So she was in hospital and her tonsils were out, and I sat down at home and wrote her a story poem to read to her on my next visit. Later I sent it to *School Magazine* and they printed it. I know now, of course, that "Raindrops" isn't really a very good poem, but we thought we should put it in the book just because it was the very first. At the time I wrote it, I'm afraid, I was very proud of it, and wrote children's verse furiously for months afterwards.

Anyone reading through this collection could not but notice how different is the first section from the two that follow. The reason is simple. There was a gap of twelve years in between when I wrote nothing at all. When I did begin again I had grown into a different person, with a much better idea of what poetry is all about. The world around me was different, too. Fairies and pixies were no longer so popular. What readers wanted, we were told, was reality, vigour and humour. And my audience had changed; my children were growing up, and one by one were moving out of my home into homes of their own. Then the grandchildren began to arrive, and presently they were clamouring for me to write for them, too. You can find Ruth and William and Rachel in this book, and there are others who are not named.

All the same, there are threads running through all three sections that bind them into a unity. From the very start I have been fascinated by rhythm and its infinite variety of patterns; not rhythm for its own sake, but rhythm so appropriate to its subject that everything is said twice over — in the sound of the words as much as in their meaning. So you have the strong "one, two; one, two" of "Down the Sandhills"; the "Red Cows", whose "slow, wise heads all gravely turn"; the quick, heavy hammering of "Wood-chop"; the hilarious scampering of "Hills", and the calm and quietness of "I Shall Buy a Farmhouse".

Then, too, the final poem of each section is particularly personal to me. "Cicada" is somehow symbolic of my own striving to emerge into an identity of my own. "Ferris Wheel", under its image of wheel and tree, has a deeper level again; of my own growth through motherhood and responsibility, to some small peak of achievement. And last of all, "Lorikeet" tells something of the way a poem comes to be written; by your looking and watching intensely until you arrive at the true essence of a thing, and then sharing your perception, your experience, by putting it into words that can make it memorable.

This book has taken forty years to write. Now I offer it to you — to children of every age, in the hope that each one of you may find in it something especially right for yourself.

Lydia Pender

FROM
MARBLES
IN MY POCKET

MARBLES IN MY POCKET

Marbles in my pocket!
Winter-time's begun!
Marbles in my pocket
That rattle when I run!

Heavy in my pocket
On the way to school;
Smooth against my fingers,
Round and hard and cool;

Marbles in my pocket,
Blue and green and red,
And some are yellow-golden,
And some are brown instead.

Marbles in the playground,
Big and little ring —
Oh, I like playing marbles,
But that's a different thing.

Marbles in my pocket,
Smooth within my hand,
That's the part that's nicest;
Do you understand?

Marbles in my pocket,
To rattle when I run!
For winter days are here again,
And marble-time's begun!

AFTER THE RAIN

I wonder, when the rain is past,
And I'm allowed outside at last,
Why all the garden seems to look
Like pictures in a picture book.

The colours all look flat and light,
Like paint-box colours, shiny-bright;
With every flower-face washed quite clean,
And every leaf a greener green,

While all the boughs are black as ink.
In fact it looks, I really think,
As if God took his paint-box out
To paint the colours all about;

For all the blues are bluer yet,
And see! His paint is still quite wet!
Oh yes, indeed, I'm sure it looks
Like children's coloured picture books.

SOAP-SUDS

When I get into the bath at night,
I lather the soap, and I lather it white.

(Why does it come white, when the soap is green?)
I lather myself most beautifully clean.

And I fill up the bath with a soapy froth,
Billowing white as a tablecloth.

Then I pull out the plug, and away it goes,
Swirling and gurgling round my toes;

(It's a wonderful noise, but it makes me shiver)
And down it rushes to join the river.

When I go to town on the boat next day,
I watch the following waves at play,

And I think, as I see them billowing white —
"There are the suds that I made last night."

RED COWS

Red cows that line the dusty road
    Along my way to school;
There where the clustered gum-trees shed
    A patch of shadowed cool;

You lift your slow, wise heads and stare,
    Knee-deep among the grass.
I know you would not harm me; still,
    I wish I need not pass.

As I trudge on, with whistled tune
    To keep my courage high,
Your slow, wise heads all gravely turn,
    To watch me passing by.

Till, as I reach the bend, and see
    The school-house, square and plain,
You drop your slow, wise heads to graze
    The shadowed grass again.

PIXIE

Down to a lily-pond,
Laughing and frolicking,
Riding the wind came a pixikin wee;
Dropped to a lily-leaf,
Light as a thistledown,
Never a ripple, a ripple made he.

Green as a grasshopper,
Red as a ladybird,
Brown as a locust-shell hung on a tree;
Winged like a dragon-fly,
Gay as a butterfly,
Nimble and fleet as a swallow was he.

Poised on a lily-leaf,
Light as a thistledown,
Softly he knelt, his reflection to see;
Laughing with happiness,
Loving his loveliness,
"Oh, you sweet fellow, sweet fellow," sang he.

Swift he was gone again,
Riding the wind again,
Dipping and twisting in frolicsome glee;
Green as a grasshopper,
Red as a ladybird,
Brown as a locust-shell hung on a tree.

BICYCLE SONG

The road is long, and the world is wide,
And the cool, fresh dawn is the time to ride.
The whirring wheels are humming a song,
And my feet beat time as I pedal along.

Where are you going? Why, I don't know —
Wherever the winding road may go.

Oh, what could equal the breathless thrill
Of a swift, mad coast down a plunging hill?
The flickering fences by my side
Go sliding backward as down I glide.

Where are you going? Oh, what care I,
While the road is smooth, and the sun is high?

I shout to the white clouds streaming past —
"I dare you up there to travel as fast!"
And I challenge a bird on the telegraph wire
Which of us two will be first to tire.

Where are you going? Oh, what care I,
While the wheels whirr on, and the sun is high?

I lift my face to a flutter of rain,
That stings my cheeks with a strange, sweet pain;
And my head is bare to the rushing breeze,
That lifts my heart to the tossing trees.

Where are you going? Why, I don't know;
I'll be home again when the sun is low.

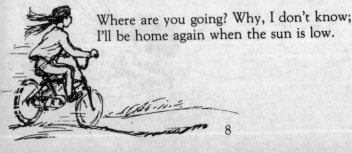

NOVEMBER

Locust-time is back now;
Through the throbbing sky
Shrill, shrill, shrill, shrill,
Rings the locusts' cry.

Eager in the tree-tops,
Shouting girl and boy
Hunt the whirring playthings,
Summer's dearest toy.

Children in the she-oaks,
Careful, lest you fall!
As shrill, shrill, shrill, shrill,
Rings the locusts' call.

FAIRIES DANCE
BY DAY

Fairies only dance at midnight,
So the fairy-stories say;
Here upon the sparkling river
I can see them dance by day.

Have you watched the windswept water,
When each wave-tip, full of fun,
Glitters like a brand-new sixpence,
Polished by the morning sun?

Surely here are fairies shining,
Nothing else could move so fast;
Scintillating, dazzling whiteness,
Ever dancing, dancing past.

Swifter than the eye can follow,
Here across the scene they spill.
Have you watched the raindrops falling?
These come crowding closer still.

Did you ever count the blossoms
On a pear tree in the spring,
When the morning throbs with music
Till you cannot help but sing?

Have you seen the dandelions
On a hillside in the sun,
Gleaming gold as scattered sovereigns?
Could you count them, every one?

Did you ever take a fistful
Of the honey-yellow sand;
Count the tiny grains that trickle
Through the fingers of your hand?

You can count till you are weary,
Till your aching eyes are sore;
Fairy thousands still unnumbered
Pirouette from shore to shore.

Fairies only dance by moonlight,
So they say, when day is done;
But I watch them on the water,
Dancing, dancing in the sun.

PLAYING SCHOOLS

When we play schools, my dolls and I,
Rebecca never seems to try.

It always seems Rebecca's fate
To have to answer — Six times eight?

And even if I thought all night
I couldn't make her answer right,

While Caroline gets — Twice times two?
And all the easy sums to do.

Ameliaranne is asked to spell
Such simple words as "good" and "well".

But when Rebecca's turn comes round,
They're long and hard, like "underground".

But still I always love her best,
Though she can't answer like the rest.

She is my dearest, 'cos you see,
She makes the same mistakes as me.

IF I WERE QUEEN

If I were Queen, and wore a crown
    Upon my head;
And no one dared to say, "Suzanne,
    It's time for bed";

If I could wear my party frocks
    Just any day;
And p'raps invite another queen
    To come and play;

Or even ask an Admiral
    To stay to tea!
If I were Queen of all the land,
    Then who'd be me?

DOWN THE SANDHILLS

A giant I stride
In the sun's hot glow,
While the pygmies play
On the beach below.

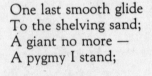

With the gulls I ride,
As with headlong bound
My seven-league boots
Swift cover the ground.

I laugh in my pride
With a fierce delight
As the beach comes leaping
To meet my flight.

One last smooth glide
To the shelving sand;
A giant no more —
A pygmy I stand;

As dwarfed by the side
Of the height whence I flew,
I turn and clamber
To soar anew.

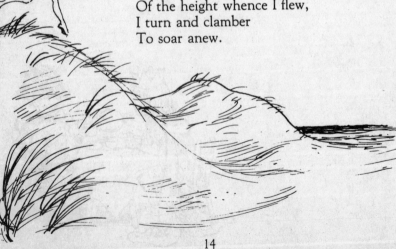

SPLASHING THROUGH
THE PUDDLES

Splashing through the puddles, when
The day is rainy-wet,
Sally finds the greatest fun
She has thought of yet.

Sally has a waterproof,
Long and green and thin,
With a little hood that ties
Underneath her chin.

When the rain is pouring down,
Off comes each small shoe;
Sally paddles through the wet
Like the ducklings do.

Standing in the gutter, where
Swift the current flows,
Rushing like a cataract
Over ten pink toes;

Though the water's icy-cold,
Sally doesn't care;
Sally's always happiest
When her feet are bare.

Splashing through the puddles when
The day is rainy-wet;
Oh! It's just the grandest game
Sally's thought of yet!

RAINDROPS

Round as green plates below the sheltering trees,
Nasturtium leaves stirred in the gentle breeze,
And raindrops, bright as quicksilver, slid round
And off the tilted leaves, upon the ground.

There a goblin, stooped and bent,
And grumbling softly as he went,
Was poking raindrops in a sack
Of cobweb thread, upon his back.

"Tell me, little man,
If you will and can,
Why you spend such care
On what you're gathering there.
Why stow them in the pack
Upon your weary back?
They're only rain, you know,
What makes you prize them so?"

He twitched his little nose in swift alarm,
As bunnies do, and with a bunny's charm;
Then, putting down his load, he answered me,
With scorn at my absurd stupidity —

"Why, some we give to water sprites
In ocean caverns deep.
They harden them and polish them,
While lazy mortals sleep;
Then tuck them into oyster shells
Where cool green water curls,
And dusky divers seek them out.
Of course, you call them pearls."

"Tell me, little man,
If you will and can,
Don't they ever drop?
Shatter with a pop?"
"In mortal hands they might,
Fairy hands are light,
Gentle, soft as smoke,
Never bubble broke.

"And some we keep for pussies' eyes,
That gleam with silver light.
The green of the nasturtium leaves
Still shines through them at night.
And some, the little bouncy ones,
The pixies keep for balls;

And fairy children love to chase
Them down the waterfalls."

"Tell me, little man,
If you will and can —"
"No more questions now,
That I can't allow.
Every baby breeze
Playing 'neath the trees,
Sends them, all around,
Splashing to the ground.

"We need each raindrop we can find
For goblins underground.
They make them into crystal lamps,
To light them on their round.
And some we keep for goldfish bowls,
Where fairy fishes swim.
You see, they are already filled
With water to the brim."

A playful breeze set all the leaves a-quiver.
They moved like wavelets on a sun-splashed river.
The last bright drops went sliding to the ground,
And the wee elf was nowhere to be found.

18

FEATHER MOON

High up in the heavens,
As sweet as a song,
A little white feather
Is drifting along;

So pale and so tiny,
So wispy and small,
You scarcely would notice
My feather at all.

Oh, little moon-feather,
You're lost, I can see.
I'll blow you back home
Into just-after-tea.

And if you are wise,
You will know that it's true,
The daytime, my darling,
Is no place for you.

For a good little moon,
So my grandmamma said,
Should never get up
Till the sun's gone to bed.

TEA-PARTY

Doll's-house folk are very small,
Not like you and me at all.

Doll's-house Mummy stiff and straight,
Doll's-house Daddy sleeping late.

Doll's-house children, fat and round,
Always tumbling on the ground.

Doll's-house Mummy says to me,
"Farmer's wife is here to tea.

Please make doll's-house Daddy stand.
Farmer's wife is rather grand."

Doll's-house tea is neatly laid.
See the cake that Mummy's made!

Doll's-house Daddy's tall and still,
Propped against the window-sill.

Doll's-house Mummy, sweet and proud —
"Children, do not speak too loud!"

Farmer's wife enjoys her tea,
Beams at all the company.

Eats her cake and sandwich up.
"Thank you, yes, another cup."

Doll's-house doggy eats the scraps
From the doll's-house people's laps.

Tea is done and cleared away —
"Do please come another day."

Off, with basket on her arm,
Trips the lady from the farm.

Doll's-house Daddy's fallen flat,
Right on top of doll's-house cat.

Doll's-house children, in a heap
On the floor, are fast asleep.

Only doll's-house Mummy stands,
Straight and still, with folded hands.

Smiles, and nods her pretty head,
"Doll's-house folk, it's time for bed."

CLICKETTY-CLACK

Hoppitty, skippitty,
Skippitty, hop.
'Way down my garden, with never a stop,
A little brown grasshopper flickered along,
And his little brown legs made a clicketty song.

Skippitty, hoppitty,
Hoppitty, skip,
Brown as a twig, and as dry as a chip.
And this is the queer little clicketty song
That the grasshopper made as he flickered along.

"Clicketty, clacketty,
Clacketty, click.
I haven't much time, so I'll have to be quick.
Clacketty, clicketty,
clicketty, clack,
As soon as I'm there, well, I'll have to come back."

'Way down the garden,
And over the gate.
(He had to be quick, or he might have been late.)
I listened all day for his clicketty-clack,
I waited all day, but he never came back.

Was he a grasshopper?
Was he an elf?
That's what I'm asking and asking myself.
Was he an elf who went skipping along,
Singing his queer little clicketty song?

"Clicketty, clacketty,
Clacketty, click.
I haven't much time, so I'll have to be quick.
Clacketty, clicketty,
Clicketty, clack.
As soon as I'm there, well, I'll have to come back."

GOOD-MORNING

Each morning, as I lie in bed,
The sun comes streaming round my head,
And wakes me up, and seems to say,
"Here comes another happy day."

I think that I should hate to miss
The smiling sun's good-morning kiss,
Or, from the camphor-laurel tree,
The birds' good-morning song to me.

I hope, when I am old and wise,
With smiling-wrinkles round my eyes,
I'll still sleep in some lovely place,
To wake with sunshine on my face.

TRAFFIC

"Stop, look, listen!"
That's what the p'licemen say,
'Cos a big one came and told us
At our little school today.
"Stop, look, listen!
For the traffic's very fast!
Stop, look, listen!
Are you sure that that's the last?"
For the proper thing to do,
When you're small, and young, and new,
Is to stop, look, listen,
Until every one is past.

But he says it much too quickly,
And he muddles me, you see.
For you can't think *very* quickly,
When your brain is only three.
"Stop, look, listen!
Till that motor car is gone;
Stop, look, listen!
For that milk-cart that you heard!"
But the way I like it said,
In my own small, quiet head,
Is — "Stop! ... Look! ... Listen!"
With a space across each word.

So I always tell my dollies,
When they cross our 'tending street —
"Stop! ... Look! ... Listen!
Before you move your feet!
Stop, look, listen!
Till that 'normous bus is past!
Stop, look, listen!
For that motorbike you heard!"
And I say it very slow,
'Cos they're little, too, you know.
"Stop! ... Look! ... Listen!"
With a space across each word.

MAKING CLOUD

When I get up for my shower each day,
I have the jolliest game to play.

The window's shut, and the gas is high,
And the steam goes whirling, curling by.

The bathroom mirror is blurred with steam,
And my face peers out, like a face in a dream.

Up to the ceiling, and out to the wall,
The eddying mist is covering all.

Then I open the window, and watch it fly,
Whirling, curling, up to the sky.

I dance with glee, and I shout aloud —
"Isn't it fun to be making cloud!"

And I count the clouds in the sky, and say —
"Seventeen boys had showers today!"

THE LIZARD

There on the sun-hot stone
Why do you wait, alone
And still, so still?
Neck arched, head high, tense and alert, but still,
Still as the stone?

Still is your delicate head,
Like the head of an arrow;
Still is your delicate throat,
Rounded and narrow;
Still is your delicate back,
Patterned in silver and black,
And bright with the burnished sheen that the
    gum-tips share.
Even your delicate feet
Are still, still as the heat,
With a stillness alive, and awake, and intensely aware.

Why do I catch my breath,
Held by your spell?
Listening, waiting — for what?
Will you not tell?
More alive in your quiet than ever the locust can be,
Shrilling his clamorous song from the shimmering tree;
More alive in your motionless grace, as the slow
    minutes die,
Than the scurrying ants that go hurrying busily by.
I know, if my shadow but fall by your feet on
    the stone,
In the wink of an eye,
Let me try —
Ah!
He's gone!

GOLDFISH

Oh lovely fish with golden sheen,
Among the water-grasses green,
Beside your glassy cage I stand
And watch you, from another land.
If I were beautiful like you
I think I'd dance the whole day through;
But though you're decked in flowing grace,
You always wear a sulky face.
I'd love to teach you how to smile;
Do try, for just a little while.

Oh fishes, don't you ever sleep?
I wait and wait, then softly peep;
But still, with solemn dignity,
You stare, unblinking, back at me.
Perhaps you slumber through the night,
But wake when I switch on the light.

I knelt one day beside a pool,
To watch its depths all dark and cool;
But saw my own small face instead,
With water-lilies round my head.
For you, it's just the other way —
Above your head reflections sway.
Another fish floats down to you,
His big, round eyes wide open too.

And like Narcissus in the lake,
You love the image that you make;
I know, I watch you rise and swim,
And lift your golden lips to him.

I bring you frog-spawn for your tea
(I'm very glad it's not for me)
And on the surface there it floats,
A hundred little jelly boats,
With one black boatman to each craft.
(I told my Daddy, but he laughed.)

I press my nose against the glass,
Between the trailing ribbon-grass;
And peering up, the water through,
Pretend that I'm a goldfish, too.
Tell me, do you wish *you* could be
Another little child like me?

THERE ARE
BUNNIES ABOUT

There are bunnies about!
Oh! There are bunnies about!
I can see two long ears poking out
From the blackberries' shelter,
And the tip of a soft little nose!
He's coming quite near!
Don't move!
    Oh, don't move, or he'll hear!
He's seen us,
    And off, helter-skelter
Just watch how he goes!

Oh, it's fun and it's fun,
When the day's just begun,
To get dressed and go out
When you know there are bunnies about!

JOIE DE VIVRE

A little green pixie sat out on a twig,
The gum-nut beside him was nearly as big;
And holding on tightly, in case he should fall,
He sang, and he sang, about nothing at all.

He cried, "I'm so happy I just have to sing,
I always feel gay when the year's at the spring,
But I will not be bothered with words to my song.
I'll copy the birds, and I cannot go wrong."

He warbled and whistled high up in his tree.
No bird sang a merrier ditty than he.
He whistled and warbled the whole of the day,
And nothing at all was the theme of his lay.

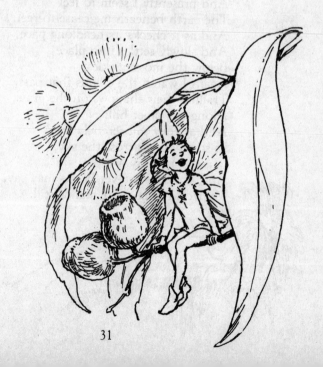

CLOUDS

Flat on my lazy back I lie
And watch great clouds go sweeping by
In endless line across the sky,
Until, until . . .
It seems to me,
It is the clouds themselves are still,
While under me the grassy hill
Is reeling giddily.
With frantic hands I clutch the ground,
While all the earth goes sweeping round,
And leaves the clouds behind.
And all geography comes true,
The world spins round, and takes me too,
And no one seems to mind.
At last I close my dizzy eyes . . .
And presently I seem to feel
The earth beneath me cease to reel;
And as it checks its headlong pace,
And slowly settles into place
Below the moving skies,
Again I watch the clouds that pass,
Trailing their shadows on the grass,
Along my quiet hill;
And as they sail serenely by
In stately line across the sky,
I cast geography away,
And know, whatever books may say,
My world once more stands still.

TOADSTOOLS

Along a hidden bushland path,
Where soft leaves hushed my tread,
And fragrant bushes brushed my skirts
And met above my head;

Where moss had spread his velvet cloak
Lest I should soil my shoe;
And misty cobwebs still at noon
Were hung with morning's dew;

A clustered group of toadstools grew,
Of palest yellow-green —
Nothing more sweetly impudent
Could I have ever seen;

For every tiny pointed tip
Was speckled spicy-brown,
Like any freckled schoolboy's face,
In any pleasant town.

I think, of every lovely thing
That in the bushland grows,
The sweetest is a toadstool small,
With freckles on its nose.

DANDELION CLOCK

Softly stirring in the moonlight,
Silvered by the silver moonlight,
    Sways a dandelion clock.
Hasten, fairies, make your greeting!
Night is fading, time is fleeting!
    Tick-a-tock, and tick-a-tock!

Who comes a-hovering
Down from the sky,
To count out the hours
That go whispering by?
Grey as the mist,
And as silver as light;
Loveliest elf ever gambolled by night;
Blue as the haze
On a faraway hill;
With fluttering wings that will never be still;
Soft he comes hovering
Down from the sky,
To count out the hours that go whispering by.

Circling the flow'r,
Like a moth round a light;
Darting and dipping
In dazzling flight;
Flickering,
Wavering,
Gliding at will,
On fluttering wings that will never be still;

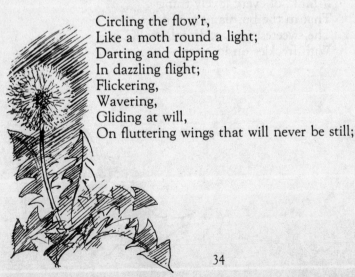

Each little cheek
Like a tiny balloon,
As he puffs at the flow'r by the light of the moon.
"One o'clock!
Two o'clock!"
See how they fly!
Feathers of thistledown under the sky!

"Three o'clock!
Four o'clock!"
Soon to be day!
Sudden he turns
And goes flitting away.
Blue as the haze,
And as silver as light;
Frisking and turning
In sheerest delight;
Chasing the thistledown feathers that fly
Drifting and quivering under the sky.
On, ever on,
To a faraway hill,
On fluttering wings that will never be still.

SHADOWS
AND ECHOES

I watched my Judy dance across the grass,
    And as the sun broke through,
A shadow, like an echo of herself,
Skipped softly close behind, as echoes do.

I called my Judy's name across the glade,
    And as she checked, and stood,
An echo, like a shadow of the sound,
Skipped softly close behind, as shadows should.

CICADA

Out of my way, everyone,
Out of my way!
I'm coming up, up, up, into the world today!
The world and the sun and the sky are waiting for
me today!
Out of my way!

Ugly, misshapen, fat, with clawlike feet,
Clad in my overalls of dusty brown,
I lived my drab, dark life through lonely years,
Down in the drab, dark earth, deep down, deep down.

But watch! See!
This is the day, the day!
Why did not somebody say
Long, long ago —
Untold, how could I know
There was a world like this, over my head?
Would I have stayed in the grave? I am not dead!
Out of my way!

Who could have known such uninspiring shell
Would hold so rare, so exquisite a thing,
With jewelled head and dainty clinging feet
And patterned tracery of fragile wing?

See, I am ready to fly!
Breasting the sky!
This is worth all the dark years that I spent in
the ground.
Ah! Let me sing, sing, sing, of the glory around!
Sing till I die!

FROM
BROWN PAPER
LEAVES

CLIMBING A TREE

Up, up into the branches
    Where the wind sings,
Feeling the leaves rustle
    Like a bird's wings;

Up through the deep shade
    Into the dappled light,
Striving eagerly on
    To the beckoning height;

Grasping the firm rungs
    Of the living ladder,
Hands finding the path,
    Feet following after;

I am glad as the wind, and strong
    In pride and power!
This is my roof, my throne,
    My fort and tower!

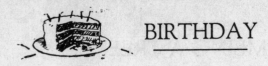

BIRTHDAY

Oh, having birthday parties is the greatest, grandest fun!
For first there's all the shopping, with balloons for everyone;

There's the lovely smell of cooking, on the day that
    Mummy bakes,
And there's scraping out the basin, when she's finished
    mixing cakes.

Then there's all the guests arriving, and the "Thank you
    very much"
For exciting-looking parcels that are knobbly to the touch;

And there's rushing round the garden in the wildest sort
    of games
With John and George and Michael, and with Christopher
    and James;

Then there's settling round the table to enjoy the party tea,
And singing "Happy Birthday" for the party boy — that's me!

(But there's a sudden funny feeling, as if someone shut a door,
That I'll never, never, all my life, be seven any more.

I was used to being seven; it's a happy age to be.
Still, eight sounds more important, for a grown-up boy
    like me.)

Then there's lighting all the candles. That's important,
    don't you think?
And the 'normous breath to blow them out, as quick as
    you could blink.

And when the fun is over, and the guests all have to go,
There is "Thank you for the party" and "I did enjoy it so".

There's a great big hug for Mummy, when the last good-byes
    are said,
And a sleepy little birthday boy is climbing into bed.

TWO THOUGHTS
ABOUT WAVES

If sound
Is only waves that break upon my ear,
Then if I were not here,
And they must just rebound
From rock, and tree, and wall
With no one listening near,
Would there be sound at all?

Sometimes it seems to me,
Hearing the ocean waves along the shore,
That I must stay awake
For each succeeding roar,
Lest it should fail to break;
As if the sea
Could somehow feel a need
That I take heed,
Or surge no more.

VISITOR

Hop. Hop. And away!
I'm sorry, I'm sorry, I really can't stay!

A tiny green frog in a shiny wet coat
(His weskit was yellow, and yellow his throat)
With a look not unfriendly, but somewhat remote,
       Came hop, hop, hop,
Out of the garden, and in at the door,
Where the sun made a bright little pool on the floor,
And there he sat blinking. Three steps, and no more.
       Hop. Hop. Hop!

Hop. Hop. And away!
You do understand? I can't possibly stay!

And then he was off again — under the chair,
And peeping in this corner, peering in there,
With such an important and businesslike air —
       Hop. Hop. Hop!
But he came to a halt with a sad little sigh
(And was that a tear I could see in his eye?)
As if what he specially wanted to buy
Was not to be found in the shop.

Hop. Hop. And away!
I don't mean to be rude, but you know I can't stay.

His eyes were so solemn, his mouth was so glum,
That I picked him up gently with finger and thumb
And turned him around to the way he had come
       With his hop, hop, hop.
He was over the step with a swift little dash!
He was back in the garden as quick as a flash!
And he dived in the pond with a soft little splash!

Hop. Hop. And away!
(But I wish he'd been able to stay!)

44

THE SEA HAS SILKEN PETTICOATS

The sea has silken petticoats
of colours rich and grand,
With tossing white embroidery
that spreads along the sand.

My petticoats are cotton lawn,
but they have 'broidery too,
With flowers made of eyelet-holes
and ribbon threaded through.

So when I paddle by the sea,
well, what do you suppose?
I've 'broidery on my petticoats
and lace around my toes.

SCISSORS

I have a bird in my hand
With a long, thin beak,
Sharp and hard,

And I feed him with paper and rag,
A piece of string,
Or a scrap of card.

I have to take care of my fingers
And tweak them away
From his snapping grin;

He might want knuckles for tea,
Or a thin little strip
From my brown skin.

When we are cutting out boats
He stretches his bill
In a wide yawn,

And closes it carefully down,
Slowly, and smooth,
In a straight line.

But when we cut faces and legs
He nibbles and nibbles
In quick pecks,

Turning and twisting his head
This way and that,
And spilling white flecks.

This morning I offered him silk,
But he scorned the limp rag,
Refusing to bite,

And it hung from his miserable mouth
Till I laughed aloud
At his comical plight.

But cardboard! Ah, watch him with that!
He worries a box
Like a dog with a bone,

Gnawing and straining his way,
Sullen and grim,
Till the task is done.

Now I have laid him away
In the table drawer,
And quiet he lies,

But the thought of tomorrow's fun,
And of tomorrow's food,
Glints in his eyes.

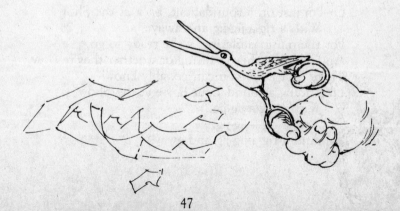

ROUNDABOUT

The roundabout horses are back at the Show,
    With a rig-a-jig-jig and away.
The music's begun, and they're rearing to go,
And the children are mounted, with faces aglow,
    With a rig-a-jig-jig and away.

I'm up on a charger that's dappledy-grey,
    With a rig-a-jig-jig and away.
His saddle and harness are handsome and gay,
And I'm hoping he'll gallop and gallop all day,
    With a rig-a-jig-jig and away.

I'll play I'm a robber, the chief of the band,
    With a rig-a-jig-jig and away.
Or I'm off to Crusades, with a lance in my hand,
To harry the Saracens out of the land,
    With a rig-a-jig-jig and away.

And now I'm a farmer that's mustering stock,
    With a rig-a-jig-jig and away.
My sheep-dogs are helping to round up the flock,
While I ride in my saddle as firm as a rock,
    With a rig-a-jig-jig and away.

Or I'm just on a roundabout, back at the Show,
    With a rig-a-jig-jig and away.
For the music is blaring, we're ready to go,
And whether they're racing or whether they're slow,
There isn't a joy you can possibly know
Like riding a roundabout horse at the Show,
    With a rig-a-jig-jig,
    And a rig-a-jig-jig,
    And a rig-a-jig-jig and away.

CHINA HORSES

White china horses
And a blue jar
On a glass table;

Story-book creatures,
Gathered from far
Legend and fable;

Little ghost horses
On the cold glass
Silent together,

Wistful of China
And of soft grass,
And crisp weather;

Frozen at play
As by a wand
Waved without warning,

Eagerly waiting
Magic's command
On a far morning;

Then will you scatter!
Canter away,
Gallop and rear!

Little white horses,
On that glad day
May I be near!

HILLS

Oh the wonderful thrill
Just to race down a hill
    When you start at the tippermost top!
Oh the glorious fun
When you've started to run,
    And you know you can't possibly stop!

Your arms are outspread,
There's a wind round your head,
    And you're certainly losing your hat!
Your heart's going thump,
And your throat's just a lump,
    Hurrah! You are down on the flat!

CAT ON THE LEDGE

Nonchalant cat
Treading the sill
Importantly fat;

Unflurried where
Dizziness reels
High in the air;

Nonchalant puss,
Picking your way
Quite without fuss

On the sheer edge
Crazily high
Of the bright ledge;

Choosing your spot
Warm in the sun,
Nor caring a jot

For frenzy and roar
Of traffic below;
You can ignore

Trifles like that,
And doze off to dreams,
Somnolent cat!

BLOODLESS BATTLE

One morning by the harbour, when the tide was very low,
A hundred little soldier crabs were marching to and fro.
    It was rather muddled drilling,
    But as everyone was willing,
They went wheeling round the muddy beach for half an
    hour or so.

There wasn't any sergeant there to tell them when to halt.
Their ranks were never very straight, but that was no
    one's fault.
    So they waved their weapons madly,
    And saluted, rather badly,
And they sometimes stopped to take a drink (but it was
    very salt).

Now drill is most exhausting work, I'm sure that you can see,
And I heard a soldier mutter, and another one agree —
    "I am tired of all this marching,
    And my throat is simply parching,
I can't stand it any longer. I must have a cup of tea!"

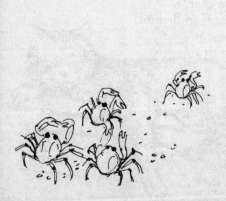

I watched him digging crazily, as if he couldn't stop,
With a hopping sort of wriggle, and a wriggling sort of hop;
    And in just about a second
    (Or as near as could be reckoned)
He had vanished quite completely, with a sudden little pop!

They didn't have a general, to tell them where to go.
They all looked most courageous, but they couldn't find
    the foe.
    Though they scuttled off to battle
    With a military rattle,
Just what they should be fighting for, they didn't seem
    to know.

So fifty little soldier crabs went marching round and round,
And the crackle of their armour made a brave and
    martial sound;

But their ranks were growing thinner
For a lot were having dinner,
And every now and then another soldier went to ground.

It was just a little later, as the tide began to rise,
That the last remaining soldier crab grew tired of exercise;
So he waved a claw, and burrowed
In the sand his mates had furrowed,
While his last defiant crackle echoed bravely to the skies.

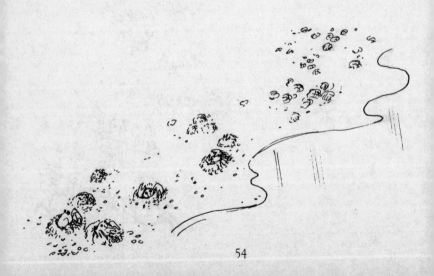

BOY

Shout! Shout, just for the joy of it!
Shout! You're a boy, and the morning is new!
Whistle your dog up, and run for the fun of it!
    Laughter's for you!

Shout! Shout, just for the heart in you,
Racing your collie-dog under the sky!
Yours is the world, and the morning's a part of you
    Galloping by!

FANTASY

The moon hung trembling in the fir;
As I passed by I saw it stir
And slip its silver beauty free
To float above the silver sea.

A sudden fancy made me fling
Up to the moon a fancied string,
To hold the end within my hand
And dance along the silver sand.

Around my happy feet, the sea
Came swirling in, to play with me,
And ever on its flimsy thread
The bright moon followed overhead.

"Hush!" sang the sea, and all along
The whispering waves took up the song,
And "Hush, oh hush!" I heard them sigh,
A never-ending lullaby.

Trailing the moon my captive still,
Gently I drew it home, until
Leaving the sand, I brought it back
To the tall trees beside the track.

In the same fir, but higher now,
It trembled on the topmost bough,
While fancy snapped the fancied thread,
And bade me take myself to bed.

BLUE WREN

What's that fluttering around my bushes?
Is it a butterfly? Oh,
So blue, so black, so quick, so bright!
But no,
See, it's a bird! Look how he brushes
Between the leaves! So small,
So blue, so black, and so light, so light!
Butterfly bird,
Do you weigh anything at all?

BROWN PAPER LEAVES

Rustling through the fallen leaves
On an autumn day,
Oh, it's such a happy game
For little boys to play!

Billy knows a shady spot
Where the plane trees grow,
And when the leaves come tumbling down
That's the place to go.

Paper leaves, that's what they are!
Such a toasty brown!
Like the stuff the parcels wear
That Mummy brings from town.

How they crackle, how they snap!
What exciting noise!
And how they tickle round the legs
Of laughing little boys!

Toss the paper armfuls high!
Watch them while they fall!
Autumn brings some lovely games,
But this is best of all.

BUTCH

Butch is a dog
Of peculiar kind,
For he's cattle before
And collie behind.

So he's never quite sure,
As he stirs in his sleep,
If he's running with cattle
Or dreaming of sheep.

THEOPHILUS JOHN

A tortoise, whose name was Theophilus John,
Had a rule which he always insisted upon,
That when he'd a journey he wanted to make,
He must first find the number of steps it would take.

Now a tortoise, of course, is exceedingly slow;
An inch at a step is the most he can go.
And an inch at a step, to go lumbering on,
Is the most to expect from Theophilus John.

One morning, Theophilus wanted a drink,
So he took out his pencil, and started to think.
"From here to the pond is exactly a yard.
I must work out the steps (and it's going to be hard).

"Now three times a yard gives the number of feet,
So I'll write down a three at the top of the sheet.
And the next thing to do is reduce it to inches.
(The worst of a tortoise-shell is that it pinches)."

He wrote down an x for the "multiply by",
And a twelve, for the inches. His throat was so dry,
And his shell was so tight; but he worked it all out.
"It's thirty-six steps!" he exclaimed with a shout.

But just as he started to waddle along,
He suddenly knew that the answer was wrong.
"For I've two pairs of feet. That is one thing I know;
I counted them, only a fortnight ago.

"Four feet must be moved. So the working is plain."
He blinked at the sky, and he wished it would rain.
"It's *four* thirty-sixes, to walk up the street;
And the answer's ... a hundred and forty-four feet."

A tear glistened wet on Theophilus' cheek.
"I'll be working it out till the end of the week!
If only my home had a kitchen and sink,
I could turn on the tap, and have water to drink!"

Then a wonderful notion took hold of his brain.
He snatched up his paper and pencil again,
And he wrote to the agent who lived down the road,
"Could you find for me, please, a convenient abode?

"I have to get rid of this troublesome shell,
For it's horribly cramped, and it's draughty as well;
And I MUST HAVE A HOUSE WITH THE WATER
    LAID ON.

Signed,

very sincerely,

Theophilus John"

HAILSTORM

Then came the hail. Taking us by surprise
Thousands of hailstones spilled down out of the skies,
Bouncing and skipping and dancing like children at play,
Dropping and nestling into the grass like clover,
Like mushrooms, in great drifts of white.
Oh, what a *joyous* sight!

And it was over. But immediately after,
Out poured the children, bubbling with laughter,
Spilling out of their houses, over their lawns,
Gathering hailstones, gathering mushroom hailstones,
Skipping and dancing with delight.
Oh, what a *joyous* sight!

SAILOR-BOYS

Ten little sailor-boys are clinging to the rigging
(The wet sails are flapping, and tugging at the mast),
And ten little sailor caps, in spite of all their jigging,
Stick tightly to their little heads, as the wind streams past.

Tell me, little sailor-boys, the answer to my guesses,
Why your little sailor caps never blow away?
We're only wooden clothes-pegs, to hold your
    pretty dresses,
Blowing in the sunshine of your mother's washing-day!

GIANTS

How would *you* like it —
Supposing that *you* were a snail,
And your eyes grew out on threads,
Gentle, and small, and frail —
If an enormous creature,
Reaching almost up to the distant skies,
Leaned down, and with his great finger touched
    your eyes
Just for the fun
Of seeing you snatch them suddenly in
And cower, quivering, back
Into your pitiful shell, so brittle and thin?
Would you think it was fun then?
Would you think it was fun?

And how would *you* like it,
Supposing you were a frog,
An emerald scrap with a pale, trembling throat
In a cool and shadowed bog,
If a tremendous monster,
Tall, tall, so that his head seemed lost in mist,
Leaned over, and clutched you up in his great fist
Just for the joy
Of watching you jump, scramble, tumble, fall,
In graceless, shivering dread,
Back into the trampled reeds that were grown so tall?
Would you think it a joy then?
Would you think it a joy?

CHRISTMAS BEETLES

Bumping their silly heads against the wall,
    Here come the clowns again!
The Christmas clowns, to poke their happy fun
    And banish frowns again!

Here is the circus in your sitting-room.
    Such crazy tumbling!
See how they race, and butt their heads, and fall
    With studied fumbling!

Those intermittent bursts of foolish buzz
    Are jokes for certain!
Welcome them in. This is the turn we love.
    Ring up the curtain!

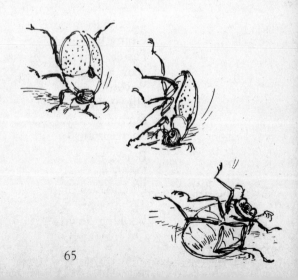

BIRD'S-EYE VIEW

High
At an office window, I
Look down
And see the crown
Of a flat
Round hat
Go by.

Far below,
The heel and toe
And the flat
Round hat
Are all I see.
(Don't fall,
They say to me.)

Then another
And another,
Out they come
In a smother,
For it's five
And from the hive
They all come pouring out
And swirl about,
Going home.
Faster, faster,
Man and master,
Boy and girl,
Hurry, hurry,
Such a scurry,
Such a whirl!

But to me,
Don't you see,
Perched up high;
To my eye
Looking down
On the town;

All the crowd,
Poor or proud,
Are only heads,
Hats and heads,
Going by.
Just their feet
Come and go
On the street
Far below.
Just their feet
Brown or black
Come and go
Front and back,
And carry the hats,
Carry the heads,
Home to their flats,
Home to their beds,
Whether or no.

It's nearly night.
They close the window tight.
And, Down you climb,
They say,
For it's time
To come away.

And now, on the sill
High above,
Grey and still,
A dove
Looks down on me.
Looks down to see
Just the crown
Of my flat
Round hat,
And my own two feet
As they go,
Heel and toe,
On the street,
And carry *my* head
Back home to bed.

SURFER

To race down the slope of the sand with a shout, and
    to plunge
In the welcoming wave!
The joy, oh the joy
Of the shock of the cold, and the surge and the pull
    and the thrust
Of the buffeting sea!
To break through to air
With a gasp, and a shake of the wet from your hair,
Then down again, down —
Under the tumult that rushes above you
And under again
Till the sand drops away from beneath you and
    turning, you wait
For the greatest, the ultimate thrill!
To climb to the crest
And to yield yourself, body and will,
To the breaker that lifts you and hurls you,
    triumphant, along —
Back, back to the beach that comes leaping to meet
    your advance!
To be one with the wave!
Exultant, to live with its life, and leaving it
Live with its fellow, the following billow!
For hour after hour, for day after glorious day,
You are fish, you are man, you are thundering wave,
    you are spray!

For William Stanhope

MOUNT WARNING

It was William's birthday, the day that we climbed
    the mountain,
The six of us children, and Daddy of course, and Mother;
Clambering over the last steep slope of the mountain,
And resting, and climbing again, one helping the other.

We spread out the birthday tea on the top of the mountain,
And lit the eight candles, bright as our birthday smiles.
They shone like a crown on the head of the beautiful
    mountain,
"And people can see them," said William, "for hundreds
    of miles."

WOODCHOP

There's a sound that calls
To the bush tracks
— The steady thud
Of the swung axe.

The city crowds
To the tiered stands,
While the bushmen wait
With quiet hands.

Then the sun glints
On the flung blade,
And strong and sure
Are the strokes made.

The shaft swings
In the firm grip
To the rending tear
Of severed chip.

Tense and still
The crowd sits
Till the final blow,
When the log splits

And the city's din
Comes flooding back;
But the scent of the cleft wood
Is the scent of the track.

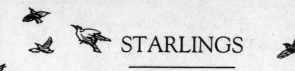

STARLINGS

Like crumbs from someone's shaken tablecloth,
A score, at least, or more
Of speckled starlings drop upon the grass,
And seek, with nimble beak,
To snatch at every dainty that they pass.

They move in concert, picking as they go,
Precise, efficient, and concise;
Then weightless, effortless, lift, and fluttering fly,
A cloud of birds, into the cloudless sky.

RUTH IS TWO

Ruth drew a letter-box
(I knew it was a letter-box)
Ruth drew a letter-box
And Ruth drew a cat.

And Ruth drew
A letter too,
To drop into the letter-box.
Now who would think so small a girl
Could draw so much as that?

HARBOUR BY NIGHT

When harbour tides ebb low
The prawners come. In husky voice and slow
I hear them, each to each,
Tossing their whispered words along the beach.

Dark forms wade deeply by,
And phosphorus furs with silver leg and thigh.
The crescent net's aflame,
Shivering with icy fire, to the stars' shame.

With swinging lamp in hand
One moves with sober tread across the sand,
While with eccentric stride
His huge, fantastic shadow jerks beside.

And in the deep-piled tin,
Scratching and scrabbling with a panic din,
Their hot, red eyes agleam,
The frenzied captives seek their ravished stream.

SCOOTER

Who comes speeding down the street?
— Two round wheels,
And two small feet,
And two tight hands to steer the way?
It's me!
And here I come!
Hooray!

HONEY-EATER

Among the fuchsia flowers
In the fresh morning hours,
She hangs on whirring wings,
Doing amazing things!

Thin beak pressed up
Into the scarlet cup,
She sips each vivid cluster
All in a merry fluster!

Now here, now there,
She hovers in mid-air —
And off — who could have stopped her,
My frenzied helicopter!

SKY

Isn't the sky blue, blue, blue today!
So blue, there's nothing more I need to say
But — Oh, isn't it *blue!*

PULLING SCRUB:
QUEENSLAND

They're pulling scrub in the brigalow belt, and
    toppling down the trees,
And the tractors rage through the brigalow scrub
    like ships through the stormy seas,
With the long, long loop of relentless chain that
    is linking them each to each;
And the thud of trunks and the swish of leaves are
    like surf on an angry beach.

It's a war of the worlds in the brigalow belt when
    the monstrous tractors ride
With their thrusting visors of painted steel, and
    the sweat-stained men inside;
And I watch the trees in their turbulent wake, with
    a terrible, thundering roar,
Come crashing down into the undergrowth, like waves
    on a windy shore.

The air is thick with the hanging dust, and the field
    is strewn with dead,
But the yellow monsters have lumbered on. They are
    pulling the patch ahead.
And I know that in time the grass will grow, and the
    cattle will fatly graze,
But I shall remember the war of the worlds, and these
    wonderful, terrible days.

PIGEON-HOUSE

A pigeon-house
On a tall post
Is a thing that matters
More than most.

Take whatever
Else you may,
This place is home
While the pigeons stay.

For the sharp gleam
Of a pigeon's white
On the green grass
Is a sweet sight;

And the nodding peace
Of a pigeon's call
Is a thing that matters
Most of all.

FERRIS WHEEL

Now I know what it is like
    To grow, like a tree,
    Out of the ground!

Slowly we take on our load,
    And the chair swings free
    As the wheel turns round.

And I and the wheel are one —
    No longer a wheel,
    But a tree that grows!

Rooted and firm are my feet,
    But my brow can feel
    The wind as it blows!

As I lift, as I lift, my horizons
    Stretch and expand;
    And growth brings release

From fears that I knew, and perils
    Once closer at hand,
    For stature is peace.

There are children safe under my shade
    To cluster and move;
    And there they belong.

Where better, where better to seek
    Protection and love?
    For see! I am strong!

And now, as my summit is reached,
    There are stars in my hair!
    I am rooted, but free!

Ah, now I know how it must feel
    To grow through the air,
    To grow,
    To grow like a tree!

MORE
RECENT VERSE

THE BALL

Can you catch?
Then watch while I throw it,
Up, ever so high.
White is the ball, so white
On the blue sky.

Run now,
Run under it, quick!
It's beginning to drop —
Drawn by the pull of the ground
To your two hands' cup.

Now you throw it yourself,
Higher yet.
Will it ever come down?
Will it float like a bubble all day
Over paddock and town?

But it hangs
Like a catch in the breath
While the moment expands,
Then faster and faster it speeds
To the cup of my hands.

RUTH HAS TUMBLED

Ruth has tumbled off the bridge
(Oh, my tiny daughter!)
Cut her foot on something sharp
Underneath the water.

Doctor came and sewed it up
With neat and careful stitches;
So now she hops, and now she stops,
And dodges round the ditches.

MORNING MAGPIE

"King Richard the First,"
  Sings the magpie. He burst
Into song at the rise of the sun.
  Now he sings and he sings
  Of all manner of things,
And I know that the morning's begun.

"King Richard the First,"
  Sings the magpie. He burst
Into song as I wakened in bed.
  Fly down to my lawn,
  You bird of the dawn,
Oh, come down to the grass and be fed.

DITCHDIGGERS

Like lean giraffes about the building site,
With questing noses tilted to the sky,
They stand, a still and silent little herd,
And let the world go by ...

Until the whistle blows. And then they turn
With lowered heads, travel and work and wheel,
Grabbing great gobbets of the yellow clay
To toss it into trucks, tireless as steel ...

Until the whistle blows again. And then,
With noses tilted up against the sky,
They stand, a still and silent little herd,
And let the world go by.

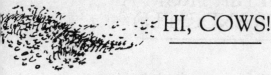

HI, COWS!

The paddock's gay with yellow flowers
    like tiny butterflies.
Hi, cows! Ho, cows!
    Look what's here for tea!

    Green grass is good enough.
    Green grass is sweet enough.
    Green grass is crisp enough.
        Grass does me.

Why stay on the river flats
    when flowers grow on the hill-top,
Fluttering like butterflies?
    (The wind is off the sea.)

    Green grass is good enough.
    Green grass is sweet enough.
    Green grass is crisp enough.
        Grass does me.

But butterflies are special food,
    are fairy food, are party food.
Hi, cows! Ho, cows!
    Won't you come and see?

    Green grass is good enough.
    Green grass is sweet enough.
    Green grass is crisp enough.
        Grass does me.

LETTER FROM A
GRANDCHILD

A Christmas letter, garlanded with stars!
What richer could I ask,
Thinking of books and toys all laid aside
For this most careful task?

Pale candles climb the margin of the page
To where the Christmas child
Lies sleeping in his mother's gentle arms,
Mary, the meek, the mild.

And all around the neatly written lines
Are more small pictures, clipped
From last year's cards, as colourful and gay
As an old monk's illumined manuscript.

SOUNDS AND SHAPES
ON A LONG BEACH

The sounds of the sea are round,
Round as the clouds
That are piled in the sky.

The shapes of the sea
Are jagged, smooth, curved
Under the eaves of the waves,
Or spread, syrupy thin,
Over the sand as the tide comes sweeping in;
With sharp, prickly spikes of sunlight
Clustered like thorns
Over its choppy surface,
Under the wheeling gulls.

The shapes of the sea
Are every conceivable shape
To baffle the eye;
But the sounds of the sea are round
As the clouds in the sky.

ROSELLA

Gaudy, incredible bird, flown in from the bush,
And trundling clumsily, heavily, over my grass,
Do you come for the water I set in the
    earthenware dish,
Or the bread that I hopefully toss?

On the ground you are awkward and old;
But oh, when you fly!
A dazzle of scarlet and gold!
And your wings are green Catherine-wheels
Aflame in the sky!

... AND RAINBOW
LORIKEETS

So very much the same
And yet, quite different still,
These much less timid birds
Perch on my window-sill,

Noses against the glass.
Surely identical twins!
Heads at identical tilt,
Wearing identical grins.

Pale collar carefully tied
Under each blue-capped head,

Smart as a party they come,
Demanding their sugar-soaked bread.

Tail-coats thoroughly brushed,
Each green feather in line,
Waistcoats, ruddy as flame,
Buffed to a glowing shine,

They fly to my gutter and cling,
Tails upward, heads hanging down,
And wink at me, sharing the joke.
Was ever more elegant clown?

Their food is set on the grass.
They drop, in a flurry of wings;
Then neatly, stiffly as toys,
They bounce on hidden springs.

Nibbling with delicate speed,
They relish their daily treat,
With a tiny fountain of crumbs
Spilling around as they eat,

Till — was it a threatening sound
Or a sudden move that I made?
— They freeze; and explode into flight.
The red-hot pokers fade.

MERRY-GO-ROUND

Electrons whirl around their core.
The earth whirls round the sun.
And galaxies swirl in and out
Like some celestial roundabout
Within the universe, no doubt,
Since time begun;
And will, they say, for evermore.
Since time began, I should have said.
The trouble is, my dizzy head
Is twirling like a crazy top.
And so this poem has to ... STOP!

RUTH IS FIVE

Ruth wrote a letter;
It wasn't very long,
But all the words were dancing
As if they sang a song.

When Mother writes a letter
It's dignified and neat.
The words sit straight upon the line
Like dolls along a seat.

But Ruth's went climbing up the page
And then came running down.
It was quite the gayest letter
That ever came to town.

SKATEBOARDS

They glide and dart about the street
Like fish along a shallow,
Weaving a pattern that the eye,
Compulsively, must follow.

Round moving reeds of trousered legs
They wind, or sharply veer
To miss a sudden obstacle,
As fish avoid a pier.

Tied to a single shape that threads
The busy waterway,
One's eyes are to that level held,
And at that level stay

Till, as it comes to rest, released
They lift — become aware
Of knees, shorts, shirt and shoulders,
A face, and a shock of hair!

FLYING FOXES

They drift down the dusk
Like sticks on a river,
Now in twos and in threes,
Now a dozen together.

Quiet as shadows
Their current is flowing,
Where from and where bound
Far outside of my knowing,

Till, passing my plum tree,
First one, then another
Are clinging, like debris
Thrown clear by the water.

And then ah, the clatter!
The frenzy of eating!
The wings of black leather
All flapping and beating!

Their day is the night;
Their night is the day;
And long before sunrise
They're prisoned away.

Nothing is left
But a leaf-littered lawn,
And fruit on the garden-bed,
Tooth-marked and torn.

EASTER SHOW

We're off to the Show!
We're hatted and coated, and ready to go!
Now, snorting with fuss,
The double-decked bus
Pulls up at the stop.
We climb to the top,
And we're off to the Show!

We're here at the gate!
The turnstiles are ticking
Their castanet clicking,
And early and late
The crowds will be bustling
And laughing and hustling;
And all the long queue
Will be breaking and merging
With joking and urging,
Oh, such a to-do!
And we're through!

Now for a moment's pause we stay
To welcome this delicious day;
To watch the people thronging in
And hear their sparrow-chatter din;
To feel excitement mounting high;
To see the flags against the sky;
Drink ginger beer to quench our thirst,
And choose what we shall visit first.

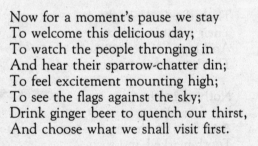

We're inside!
We're caught, and we're carried along with the tide!

And all willy-nilly,
With Beth and with Billy,
With Peter and Milly,
We follow the flow;
And whether or no
We stop when they stop
And go when they go.

Past all the decorated stands,
The demonstrators' clever hands,
A little tooting model train,
And fences made of sugarcane;
Past cooking-stoves and sandwich bars,
And brightly polished motor cars;
Until, with sample bags to spare,
We're out again in the open air.

The sideshows are calling.
Oh, hurry along!
The roundabout's churning
Calliope song.
There's the glass-blower's tent!
There's a coconut-shy!
And the ferris wheel
Clambering
Into the sky!
The pumps are all throbbing
With rhythmical sound,
And gushing green water
Is foaming and rushing
Up out of the ground.
And the windmills! The windmills

So stately and tall,
Are turning and turning,
Too proud and too busy
To see us at all!

Let's go to the ring!
Let's watch the parade!
What lunch did we bring?
Can we buy lemonade?

Shall we sit on the grass?
Shall we look for a seat?
The thoroughbreds pass
On arrogant feet.

Beribboned with pride,
Of sensitive eye,
With their owners astride,
We watch them go by.

Now round the ring a-lumbering go
The cattle, ponderous and slow,
And calves, with gentle eyes and sweet,
Follow them on unsteady feet.
The long line grows, a spiralled spring
In the packed watch-case of the ring.

But sharp and crisp
And clear and loud,
Through the din
Of chattering crowd,

The woodchop's firm
Insistent beat
Calls us in
And guides our feet

To where the axes
Thud and swing
Till the fragments fly
And the echoes ring.

Can there be even more to see?
And are we going home for tea?
The afternoon is nearly gone,
And one by one the lights steal on.
The tide has turned, and homeward bound
Drifts gently on, and eddies round
And on again, and with it we
Are carried too, reluctantly.

Beyond the gate, the crowds delay
A little while, then melt away
Like echoes of a song you've sung
Or fairy floss upon the tongue.

I SHALL BUY A
FARMHOUSE

I shall buy a farmhouse
When I've sons and daughters,
And a little creek with pebbles
And singing waters.

We shall make our home there
When we've children growing;
All our lawns shall be paddocks
And cows do the mowing.

We'll need no formal flower-beds
For tending and caring,
But a swing hung under a willow
And a mulberry bearing.

And the swooping swallows shall come
With fantastical flight
To build their nests in the eaves
For the children's delight.

Far from the smoke of the town
(I'll be glad to be going),
This is the home I shall buy
When I've children growing.

SUSIE

Susie is a darling.
Susie is my friend.
Susie's always ready
To play at Let's Pretend.

Mostly I'm the Mummy
And she's my little girl.
I brush her hair most carefully
And try to make it curl.

Susie's never whiney —
Never seems to mind
If I must go out shopping
And she is left behind.

Susie's always happy
With any kind of play;
Wakes up when I ask her,
And sleeps until I say.

Susie's just a dolly,
But somehow, in the end,
Susie is my favourite
And my *always* friend.

WHAT RACHEL SAID

My grandchild looked at my grey, grey hair.
Her eyes were round in her head.
You'll have to be dying soon, Granny,
Won't you, Granny? she said.

I'd like to be staying a wee bit longer
— If you don't mind, said I.
I've poems to write, and flowers to grow,
And it's early yet to die.

But babies have to be born, Granny!
And you've had your turn, you see.
You'll have to make room for somebody new.
But I'll miss you, Granny, said she.

CUBBY-HOUSE
IN A GARDEN

We built us a cubby of wood
With windows and door
And a roof (but no chimney, of course)
And walls, and a floor.

We fetched out our bedding and stuff,
Clive, Matthew, and me;
And tucked ourselves up for the night
Straight after our tea.

"We'll sleep here the whole of the summer!"
We were bursting with pride,
Till one said "Supposing a snake —"
And we were all back inside.

GALAHS

The tree was stark and bare; no leaf nor bud;
    Branches like bones;
No hint nor hope of any leaf to come;
    Dead as the stones.

A swirl of parrots wheel from out the sky
    And close their wings.
Magnolia flowers have burst from every bough,
    And the tree sings!

For Jemima Stehli

QUEENS AND GYPSIES

You can have the buckled shoes
And the silken shawl.
I shall wear the gypsy dress,
Beads and rags and all,

Because it's my turn to choose.

I shall walk the gypsy way,
With never shoe nor sock.
You can have the golden crown
And the flowery frock,

Because it's my choice today.

I shall sing a gypsy tune,
A raggle-taggle song.
You can sit upon your throne
The whole day long.

But it'll be your turn soon.

Today I have to beg or borrow.
Next time I'll be queen
And you will wear the gypsy dress,
Barefoot on the green,

Because it's your choice tomorrow.

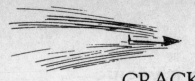

CRACKER NIGHT

As the earth turns, and as the slow sun sets,
One after one the bonfires blossom red.
Like golden water pouring up the sky
Flames splash against the blackness overhead.

Crackers and Catherine-wheels! Sparklers and
    golden rain!
Faces that glow, and vanish into dark!
Rockets that fling their sparks among the stars,
Till sparks are stars, and every star a spark!

GRANNY GROWS UP

When Granny was a little girl
    She lived in London town,
And watched the ships along the Thames
    Go steaming up and down.

But Granny lives in Sydney now,
    And she's grown old and wise.
She has a Grandpa all her own
    She feeds on apple pies.

When Granny was a little girl
    She was as good as gold.
She spoke when she was spoken to
    And did as she was told.

But now that Granny's very old
    She talks a dreadful lot.
She does just what she wants to do
    And doesn't care a jot.

When Granny was a little girl
    She wore a pinafore,
And always used her handkerchief,
    And never slammed a door.

But now that she is old and grey
    She wears the maddest clothes,
And often has a little drip
    Of water on her nose!

I wonder *was* she always good,
    Or does she just forget
The times she did the sort of things
    She really wasn't let?

RUTH IS SIX

A mobile floats above her bed
Of fishes, green and grey,
That move on drifting waves of air
As night gives place to day.

And Ruth, her eyes still dimmed with sleep,
Lies blissfully aware
Of her lazy mermaid's waving tail,
And seaweed through her hair.

JOURNEY

Up the steep air I am borne
By a monstrous bird.
No sound but our own lone sound
Can hope to be heard.

Buildings, and people, and bridges,
And a whole city, slip
Out of my vision's grasp
And my memory's grip.

Beaches are spread for my joy,
Then snatched from my sight.
Mountains are flattened to mounds
By this mad, wild height.

Soon only the rust-red plain
Extended for ever
Hour after weary hour
Yearns for a river.

Even the homestead roofs
That flashed in the sun
Have drifted from under our wings,
Diminished, and gone.

Only the seldom water-holes,
Placid and green,
Stamps stuck on an atlas, show
Where man has been.

Hour after weary hour
Till, suddenly, see!
Roads again, towns again, homes,
And a boy in a tree!

Dusk, and a city's lights —
A continent spanned —
And rest for the monstrous bird
Of this fabulous land.

CURRAWONGS

The currawongs are calling, calling
Round the nesting-tree.
The sound of their collective song
Is liquid melody.

But should one separate cruel bird
Swoop blackly to your grass,
There is no music in his cry,
And his eye is cold as glass.

STATE FOREST
IN WINTER

I walked between the rows of pines,
Each one as tall as I.
As still and straight as toys they stood,
And pointed to the sky.

As still and stiff and straight as toys
In serried lines they stood;
And I was Gulliver, and strode
A Lilliputian wood.

Their needle-leaves were tipped with ice
That caught the winter sun
And shone like tiny crystal stars.
(I picked and tasted one.)

Their needle-leaves were tipped with ice.
The wind among them crept.
They chimed like tiny silver bells,
So sweet, I all but wept.

And though July was scarce begun
I knew, and joyed to see,
Christmas was come to Lilliput
To garland every tree.

JINGLE WITH
A BALL

Throw the ball, and catch the ball,
  And throw the ball to me.
Race around the circle once
  And home in time for tea.

Catch the ball, and throw the ball,
  And round the ring again.
If you're late, we'll shut the gate,
  And leave you in the rain.

LORIKEET

He didn't look,
  and so he did not see
The parrot feeding
  in the hawthorn tree.

She looked, and saw,
  and smiled, and picked a flower,
And then forgot it
  within the hour.

Another saw,
  and watched it with delight,
And told his friend,
  and dreamed of it that night.

The last to come
  stood all entranced and stirred
By the golden berries
  and the rainbow bird;

And wrote this poem
  that all who read should see
The parrot feeding
  in the hawthorn tree.

INDEX OF
FIRST LINES